Take No Prisoners In Your Next Negotiation

How To Start A Negotiation In Order To Get The Best Possible Outcome

"Practical, proven techniques that will help you open a negotiation the right way in order to get u better deal"

Dr. Jim Anderson

Published by:
Blue Elephant Consulting
Tampa, Florida

Copyright © 2013 by Dr. Jim Anderson

All rights reserved. No part of this book may be reproduced of transmitted in any form or by any means, electronic or mechanical, including photocopying, recording or by any information storage and retrieval system without written permission of the publisher, except for inclusion of brief quotations in a review.

Printed in the United States of America

Library of Congress Control Number: 2016953608

ISBN-13: 978-1537598277
ISBN-10: 1537598279

Warning – Disclaimer

The purpose of this book is to educate and entertain. This book does not promise or guarantee that anyone following the ideas, tips, suggestions, techniques or strategies will be successful. The author, publisher and distributor(s) shall have neither liability nor responsibility to anyone with respect to any loss or damage caused, or alleged to be caused, directly or indirectly by the information contained in this book.

Recent Books By The Author

Product Management

- What Product Managers Need To Know About World-Class Product Development: How Product Managers Can Create Successful Products

- How Product Managers Can Learn To Understand Their Customers: Techniques For Product Managers To Better Understand What Their Customers Really Want

Public Speaking

- Tools Speakers Need In Order To Give The Perfect Speech: What tools to use to create your next speech so that your message will be remembered forever!

- How To Create A Speech That Will Be Remembered

CIO Skills

- Becoming A Powerful And Effective Leader: Tips And Techniques That IT Managers Can Use In Order To Develop Leadership Skills

- CIO Secrets For Growing Innovation: Tips And Techniques For CIOs To Use In Order To Make Innovation Happen In Their IT Department

IT Manager Skills

- Save Yourself, Save Your Job – How To Manage Your IT Career: Secrets That IT Managers Can Use In Order To Have A Successful Career

- Growing Your CIO Career: How CIOs Can Work With The Entire Company In Order To Be Successful

Negotiating

- Learn How To Signal In Your Next Negotiation: How To Develop The Skill Of Effective Signaling In A Negotiation In Order To Get The Best Possible Outcome

- Learn The Skill Of Exploring In A Negotiation: How To Develop The Skill Of Exploring What Is Possible In A Negotiation In Order To Reach The Best Possible Deal

Note: See a complete list of books by Dr. Jim Anderson at the back of this book.

Acknowledgements

Any book like this one is the result of years of real-world work experience. In my over 25 years of working for 7 different firms, I have met countless fantastic people and I've been mentored by some truly exceptional ones. Although I've probably forgotten some of the people who made me the person that I am today, here is my attempt to finally give them the recognition that they so truly deserve:

- Thomas P. Anderson
- Art Puett
- Bobbi Marshall
- Bob Boggs

Dr. Jim Anderson

This book is dedicated to my wife Lori. None of this would have been possible without her love and support.

Thanks for the best 21 years of my life (so far)...!

Table Of Contents

NO PRISONERS WILL BE TAKEN! 8

ABOUT THE AUTHOR 10

CHAPTER 1: THE ULTIMATE NEGOTIATION: A VERY TOUGH CUSTOMER 14

CHAPTER 2: USE THE "REVERSE-GODFATHER" APPROACH TO WIN A NEGOTIATION 17

CHAPTER 3: BIG MOUTH NEGOTIATIONS: HOWARD STERN VS. SIRIUS RADIO 20

CHAPTER 4: WHY PROVIDING A "BEST AND FINAL OFFER" IS NEVER A GOOD IDEA 24

CHAPTER 5: EVERY NEGOTIATOR NEEDS A SET OF GUIDING PRINCIPLES 28

CHAPTER 6: WHAT ROLE STATUS SYMBOLS PLAY IN NEGOTIATIONS 32

CHAPTER 7: THE ROLE THAT PHYSICAL INTIMIDATION PLAYS IN NEGOTIATIONS 36

CHAPTER 8: NEGOTIATING: MEN VS. WOMEN – WHO WANTS TO WIN MORE? 40

CHAPTER 9: TIPS FOR CONDUCTING HIGH-STRESS NEGOTIATIONS .. 43

CHAPTER 10: EXTREME NEGOTIATING: HOW TO DO YOUR BEST WHEN UNDER PRESSURE 47

CHAPTER 11: TESTING IS WHAT GOOD NEGOTIATORS DO BEST 51

CHAPTER 12: DO YOU HAVE THE PERSONALITY NEEDED FOR NEGOTIATION? 54

No Prisoners Will Be Taken!

How your next negotiation is going to turn out will be determined by how you open the negotiation. No matter if the other side is a push-over or a tough customer, you are going to have to decide how you want the negotiation to start and then you are going to have to take steps to make it happen.

What makes an opening so very important in a negotiation is that it lays the groundwork for everything else that will follow. No matter if you are planning on using the "reverse godfather" approach or just want to duke it out like Howard Stern did with his employer, you are going to have to make sure that you have a set of guiding principles that you follow.

The other side will see how you are starting out and they will work to counter you at every step. They may hit you with a "best and final offer" – will you know what to do when this happens? You have the ability to hit them back by using status symbols or perhaps even physical intimidation.

A key part of any negotiation that you open is to understand who is going to be doing the negotiating: boys or girls. This is critical because they do negotiate differently. As the pressure starts to build in your next negotiation, you are going to have to make sure that you know how to handle a high-stress negotiation.

Not every negotiation that you open will be the same. Some will be extreme and you'll have to deal with that when it happens. If you are a good negotiator, then you'll know how to use testing in order to find out what the other side is really up to. In the end, it's all going to come down to your personality. Do you really have what it takes to be a great negotiator?

For more information on what it takes to be a great negotiator, check out my blog, The Accidental Negotiator, at:

www.TheAccidentalNegotiator.com

Good luck!

- Dr. Jim Anderson

About The Author

I must confess that I never set out to be a negotiator. When I went to school, I studied Computer Science and thought that I'd get a nice job programming and that would be that. Well, at least part of that plan worked out!

My first job was working for Boeing on their F/A-18 fighter jet program. I spent my days programming fighter jet software in assembly language and I loved it. The U.S. government decided to save some money and went looking for other countries to sell this plane to. This put me into an unfamiliar role: I started to negotiate with foreign military officials and I ended up having to participate in the negotiations for large international deals.

Time moved on and so did I. I found myself working for Siemens, the big German telecommunications company. They were making phone switches and selling them to the seven U.S. phone companies. The problem was that the switches were too complicated. When it came time to negotiate a deal with the customer, the sales teams struggled to create an effective negotiating strategy. I was called in to bridge the world between the product functionality and the business impacts as they related to the negotiations.

I've spent over 25 years working as a negotiator for both big companies and startups. This has given me an opportunity to learn what it takes to both plan and execute negotiations of all sizes. When it comes to negotiations, I've pretty much been there, done that.

I now live in Tampa Florida where I spend my time managing my consulting business, Blue Elephant Consulting, teaching college courses at the University of South Florida, and traveling to work with companies like yours to share the knowledge that I have about how to prepare for and execute successful negotiations.

I'm always available to answer questions and I can be reached at:

Dr. Jim Anderson
Blue Elephant Consulting
Email: jim@BlueElephantConsulting.com
Facebook: http://goo.gl/1TVoK
Web: http://www.BlueElephantConsulting.com/

"Unforgettable communication skills that will set your ideas free…"

Create An Effective Negotiating Team At Your Company!

Dr. Jim Anderson is available to provide training and coaching on the topics that are the most important to people who have to negotiate: how can my team effectively prepare for and execute a successful negotiation that will get us what we both want and need?

Dr. Anderson believes that in order to both learn and remember what he says, audiences need to laugh. Each one of his speeches is full of fun and humor so that what he says "sticks" with everyone.

Dr. Anderson's Negotiating Training Includes:

1. How to plan for a negotiation: what information do you need and where can you find it?

2. What's the best way to explore how a deal can be created during a negotiation?

3. How can you bring a negotiation to a close without giving in to the other side?

Dr. Jim Anderson works with over 100 customers per year. To invite Dr. Anderson to work with you, contact him at:

Phone: 813-418-6970 or
Email: jim@BlueElephantConsulting.com

Chapter 1

The Ultimate Negotiation: A Very Tough Customer

Chapter 1: The Ultimate Negotiation: A Very Tough Customer

In the world of negotiations there are the easy ones (getting a discount on that lawnmower that you bought) and the hard ones (a difficult customer to whom nobody has ever been able to sell). It's the difficult customers that are the most interesting because they are a real challenge no matter what stage of negotiating you are at. Let's take a look at this type of customer and see if we can come up with a strategy that will boost your chances of successfully concluding a negotiation with them.

Negotiations with a difficult customer rarely look like a formal negotiation with both parties sitting on different sides of the table. Rather, a negotiation with a difficult customer often starts out as a discussion and then steers into negotiation territory. That's why you as a negotiator always needs to be ready to switch into negotiator mode when the customer wants to start negotiating.

One of the best things that you can do right off the bat when you are dealing with a difficult customer, says Grande Lum who is a negotiation training profession, is to take ownership of the situation. All too often customers become upset with the way things are going and they feel that nobody is stepping up to the plate in order to take charge and solve the problem. By accepting ownership of the situation and perhaps even going so far as to apologize if it is called for, you can diffuse the situation from the start.

Your next challenge is to find out why they are being difficult. There is a good chance that their motivation for being so adversarial has nothing to do with the deal that you are currently discussing. Rather, long simmering issues with you company, other people who work for your company, etc. could be spilling over into the deal that you are currently working on. Of course there is also the possibility that this is just the way that this customer deals with anyone who is trying to get him/her to buy something – it's a negotiating tactic.

Lum has come up with a clever way to deal with difficult customers which he calls the ICON framework for negotiation. ICON stands for the four steps that you need to move through during the negotiation: Interest, Criteria, Options, and No-Agreement Alternatives. When using this frame work, you first probe the customer for Interest, then you use the information gleamed from this to establish a Criteria that you can use to understand and persuade, next you brainstorm with the customer to come up with Options and finally you make sure that you identify No-Agreement Alternatives so that you have a fallback option should the negotiations not work out.

If you are looking for a magical silver bullet that will instantly solve your negotiation problems with a difficult customer, bad news – it doesn't exist. However, if you can get them engaged and get them talking and into a problem solving mode then you've succeeded in getting them working in the right process. In some cases this just is not possible with your customer. You then need to reach out to others who work at his/her company and ask for their help in understanding what is causing your negotiation problems.

Chapter 2

Use The "Reverse-Godfather" Approach To Win A Negotiation

Chapter 2: Use The "Reverse-Godfather" Approach To Win A Negotiation

In the classic movie, The Godfather, Marlin Brando utters the unforgettable phrase "I'll make him an offer he can't refuse." Clearly Brando's character Don Corleone is operating from a position of negotiating power as the head of an organized crime family. However, is there anything in this phrase that us mere mortals can use?

It turns out that, with a twist, yes there is something here for us negotiators. Specifically, what we can do is make the other side of the table an offer that they MUST refuse. Now why would you ever do such a thing?

This is a powerful negotiating tool and when used correctly it can produce amazing results. When you make an offer to the other side that you know that they just have to refuse, what you really are doing is setting the stage for when you make offers later on. These future offers will look reasonable in comparison to the offer that they refused.

During a negotiation, time is one of your most valuable tools. The more time that you have, the more power that you have. Making an offer that the other side must refuse will buy you more time that will allow you to spend it exploring additional alternatives that may end up being acceptable to both sides.

Interestingly enough, this technique can also be used to either stall the negotiations or even perhaps cause the negotiations to break down and come to a complete halt. You may want to do this if it turns out that moving the negotiations to a different time would be more favorable to you. This may allow you to create a better set of arguments that will result in a better outcome for you in the end.

If we could read the other side's mind this whole negotiation thing would go much quicker. Since (most of us) can't do this, making an offer that the other side must refuse will help you to bound the negotiations and get closer to finding out what the other side views as being an acceptable offer.

What's interesting about making a clearly unacceptable offer is that it will interrupt the flow of the negotiating conversation. When the other side starts to believe that perhaps no agreement may be able to be reached, they are often likely to drop their "negotiating face" and talk candidly with you.

This is your best chance to discover their real motivations – sorta like reading their minds. Once you have this information, then you will be well positioned to make use this knowledge to make a follow-up offer that will be much more acceptable to the other side.

Yes, yes – as with everything in life, there is some risk associated with using this technique. The other side may become so upset that they just up and walk away from the negotiations. However, using this technique carefully and in the correct negotiating situations can open up avenues to reaching a solution that were not previously available. Remember that before you use this technique, you want to make sure that you have left yourself a way to re-enter the negotiation – don't get shut out!

Chapter 3

Big Mouth Negotiations: Howard Stern Vs. Sirius Radio

Chapter 3: Big Mouth Negotiations: Howard Stern Vs. Sirius Radio

That Howard Stern is famous, nobody can deny this. That he is paid a lot of money is another indisputable fact. Where things get interesting (from a negotiating point of view) is what happens when **his current contract runs out…**

If you've ever listened to Howard for any length of time, he's always talking about his relationship with the Sirius satellite radio network. He's very grateful for everything that they've done for him and his team; however, he's recently been saying on the air: **"I don't think that I'm going to be re-signing."**

Clearly pre-negotiating posturing is already well underway. Howard is no dummy and he's got a **great way to communicate his negotiating position to the other side of the table** via his daily radio show.

Back when Sirius hired Howard away from traditional radio, satellite radio was a new kid on the block and more of a curiosity than a viable radio network However, by hiring Howard, Sirius was able to put themselves instantly into the press and brought themselves **to the attention of both new subscribers as well as investors**. Since he's been on board, Sirius has been able to add millions of new subscribers.

Howard was richly rewarded for making the jump to satellite radio – the contract that he got gave him **$500M in cash and stock** over five years.

The Posturing

The CEO of Sirius radio, Mel Karmazin, has been quoted as saying "It is my strong desire that we keep Howard in satellite radio on terms that are in the best interest of our shareholders." **Clearly Mel is also skilled at the pre-negotiating posturing game also.**

The world has changed since Sirius hired Howard five years ago — **they don't need Howard as much today as they did back then**. Sirius has been able to add other well-known talent to their lineup included most recently Rosie O'Donnell.

Now that's all good and well, but having Howard on board is a big plus for Sirius. If he were to leave, then **Sirius would probably lose subscribers**. What's interesting is that the company has changed its focus from only growth to now being more focused on profitability.

The reason that anyone can even start to talk about Howard leaving is because it's a real possibility. The cause is pretty simple — Howard's paycheck represents **a very large expense for the company.**

The Possible Outcomes

So as students of sales negotiating, what does all of this show us? Well, we've got two parties doing their best to clearly communicate their starting positions to the other side of the table before negotiations even begin. **There are a number of different ways that this could all end up.**

Although unlikely, it is possible that Howard could once again land a job on traditional airwaves. He had originally left because of the public outrage over the content of his show; however, times have changed and this might not be such a big deal any more. **The challenge of "saving" traditional radio might be more than Howard can resist.**

What All Of This Means For You

There is much for us to watch and learn from here: Howard wants to work less and make more money, Sirius wants him to work more for less money.

When negotiating starts, it's almost certain that we'll see some very **interesting posturing** occurring by both sides. Due to the public nature of Howard's job, we'll be provided with a window into the negotiations and a running commentary on how he wants us to think that he feels about the process.

Turn your Sirius radios on and get ready for some lessons in **high-stakes negotiations!**

Chapter 4

Why Providing A "Best And Final Offer" Is Never A Good Idea

Chapter 4: Why Providing A "Best And Final Offer" Is Never A Good Idea

Every sales negotiation starts out in a particular way. Sometimes it's good like when the other side lays out the issues and makes a concession to you right off the bat. Other times it's bad. You know it's going to be bad when the first words out of the other side's mouth are "Give me your best and final offer". What's a sales negotiator to do now?

Demand And Offer Tactics

In the world of sales negotiations there is a group of set tactics that have been used since the start of time. Starting a negotiation by stating that you want the other side's best offer is one of these ancient tactics.

Often times when the other side makes this bold statement, they'll follow it up with an explanation. This explanation often goes something along the lines of "I don't like to negotiate". Great statement, but it's pretty much untrue – this is simply the way that they like to start their negotiations.

Why Providing A Best And Final Offer Is Never A Good Idea

What the other side is trying to do is to get you to start the negotiations at a lower price point than you normally would. This is a fantastic advantage for them – they will have made a great deal of negotiating progress with very little effort on their part.

All too often, when a negotiator is presented with this kind of statement, they'll panic. The last thing that they want to do is to anger or upset the other side of the table and so they'll react in a way that they think will diffuse the situation. Generally this means that they'll go ahead and lower their price.

The problem with this is that despite what the other side said, the offering of this lower price does not result in a deal. Rather it just provides a point for the negotiations to start at. Once the other side sees how much you were quickly willing to come down in price, they'll know that there is more lowering that you can be made to do.

How To Counter This Negotiating Tactic

As a sales negotiator you need to be on the lookout for the use of this tactic. When the other side starts to use it on you, clearly what you don't want to do is to follow along and provide them with a low-ball offer.

Instead, what you are going to want to do is to change the discussion. Without rejecting outright what they are asking for, you're not going to want to give it to them.

What you are going to want to do is to take the time to explain why your position is so unique that it's worth the initial value that you've placed on it. Make sure that you point out things that the other side of the table can't get anywhere else.

After all of this is said and done, you may still find yourself in a position where some lowering of your price is going to be necessary. That's ok. Just make sure that you only lower it a small amount. Once again, this isn't going to allow you to reach a deal, rather it's the start of the negotiating process.

What All Of This Means For You

Every sales negotiation involves the use of tactics by both sides in order to get what they want. You will often encounter situations where the other side tells you to provide them with a best and final offer. Don't do it!

Instead, use this as an opportunity to revisit why your offering is more valuable than other offerings that may be available at a lower price. Yes, the other side will push back on this, but you will have changed the discussion from a pricing discussion to a discussion about the value of your offering. This is much safer ground.

In the end, every sales negotiation comes down to price. Being aware of the other side's tactics and making sure that you are ready to deal with them is what will make you a great sales negotiator.

Chapter 5

Every Negotiator Needs A Set Of Guiding Principles

Chapter 5: Every Negotiator Needs A Set Of Guiding Principles

Negotiations can go on for a long time. When you start a negotiation, you probably have **a pretty good idea of where you want to get to**. The big question is does the other side of the table share this goal with you? Will they be able to remember this goal throughout the entire negotiation? Hmm, sounds rather iffy to me. Perhaps what you need are a set of guiding principles...

What Are Guiding Principles In Negotiating?

So just exactly what are **guiding principles** when we are talking about the world of negotiating? Guiding principles are different from negotiation styles and negotiating techniques – they are high level agreements that you are able to reach with the other side that frame the rest of your discussions. These are an important part of any principled negotiation.

A negotiation definition requires that your negotiations focus on the details of the deal that is to be done: who gets how much, when things get shipped, where they get delivered to, terms of credit, etc. At a much higher level, these details assume that both you and the other side of the table have **come to an agreement on the big issues**.

These issues center on things like how much profit is it fair for the other side to make on the deal? How soon after the deal is signed should the other party expect to see its money? What should be done if the product or service does not live up to expectations? These are big issues that both sides need to come to an agreement on **at the start of the negotiations**.

How Do You Use Guiding Principles In Negotiating?

Having taken the time to discuss a set of guiding principles at the start of your next negotiation, **what does all of this buy you?** What it does is to buy you some insurance that the time that you invest in the negotiations won't be wasted.

By taking the time to establish some guiding principles with the other side, you've **established a beachhead** from which both sides can make progress. There's another advantage of doing this.

Negotiations can be long, drawn-out affairs and it can be easy to **lose your way** in the middle of one. For that matter, the other side can get lost also. When you have both agreed on a set of guiding principles, this provides you with a place to come back to when you get lost or the negotiations get bogged down. The guiding principles provide you with a milestone – a point where you and the other side actually did agree on something.

By having this kind of "basecamp" to come back to, the negotiations need never get off track. Sure, they may get bogged down in disagreements over details, but both sides will always **have a place that they can come back to** in order to get the negotiating process restarted.

What All Of This Means For You

Getting from the beginning to the end of a negotiating session is a lot harder than it may seem. All too often we can **lose our way** during the negotiation process and the other side of the table can get lost with us. This makes reaching a negotiated deal that much harder to do.

Establishing a set of guiding principles at the start of the negotiations is a great way to **clearly communicate** to the other side what it's going to take to reach a deal. The guiding principles will provide both sides with a base that you can come back to later on in the negotiations if either side gets lost.

It will take some time to establish a set of guiding principles at the start of the negotiation. This investment of time will **yield significant results** by helping to keep both sides of the table on track. Do it right and you'll be able to reach a deal that works for everyone involved.

Chapter 6

What Role Status Symbols Play In Negotiations

Chapter 6: What Role Status Symbols Play In Negotiations

When it comes to sitting around the negotiating table, we're all equal, right? In a perfect world, the answer would be yes. We don't live in a perfect world and so the answer is a very solid "no". So what does this mean for us – **do some negotiators deserve to get more?**

Where Negotiating Status Comes From

Where does this status thing come from? It seems to play a role in our negotiation styles and negotiating techniques. I'm pretty sure that we're all very aware of the role that social status used to play in European society back in the day. You had your upper class folks and then the rest of humanity. If an upper class negotiator sat down to negotiate with a lower class person, then they would be **starting with a huge advantage** simply because of their social status. This would undoubtedly affect the final deal that was negotiated.

Those days are long gone – or are they? In Europe, as well as in places like India, although officially the social classes have been removed, **traces still linger**. When two negotiators from two very different backgrounds sit down to negotiate, the ghosts of their family's backgrounds can at times haunt the room.

Additionally, a new type of social status symbol has arrived on the scene. A person's success in life as represented by all of the **"bling"** that comes with success – money, power, acclaim, etc. can elevate their social status. If you don't believe me, then just imagine how you would feel if you were sitting across from Donald Trump trying to negotiate a deal with him!

How You Can Deal With Status At The Negotiating Table

I'd like to be able to tell you to **just ignore status** when you are conducting your next negotiation. Focus on the deal that you're trying to create and ignore who the person that you are negotiating with is or where they come from.

That's easy for me to say and very hard for you to do! It's never going to be easy for you to overlook the other side of the table's status – it's going to affect your negotiation process. Instead, I'm going to suggest that you **do something else** that will help you to work through this issue.

In order to retain your composure when you are negotiating with someone who has more status than you, **you need to boost your status**. The easiest way to go about doing this is to do additional work preparing for the negotiations. I have found that people with status often assume that their status is going to help them to reach a deal and so they will often not do as much preparation for a negotiation as they should have. Do your homework and you'll be better prepared than they are and their status won't matter as much.

What All Of This Means For You

We do not live in a perfect world – **we are not all equal**. Instead, status and status symbols play a role in every negotiation – this is almost a part of the negotiation definition.

What this means for you as a negotiator is that you need to realize that **status can play a role in how you both view and treat the other side of the negotiating table** even when you are conducting a principled negotiation. You need to work to overcome any status advantage that they may have by working extra hard to prepare for the negotiation – you need to be the best prepared person at the table.

Status as something that **makes people different** is something that we'll always have to live with. As long as you know that this is an issue, then you can take steps to deal with it and make sure that it does not influence the deals that you make.

Chapter 7

The Role That Physical Intimidation Plays In Negotiations

Chapter 7: The Role That Physical Intimidation Plays In Negotiations

During a negotiation, you'd hope that we'd all be adults about it. Right? Well it doesn't always turn out that way. Using either **physical or environmental means to intimidate the other side is a negotiation styles or negotiating techniques that the other side of the table may use as a** common negotiating technique. You need to be aware of this before a negotiation starts so that you can come up with a way to deal with it.

Physical Intimidation During A Negotiation

Unless your sales negotiation process is taking place in some dark back alley, you wouldn't think that physical intimidation would play a role in **a modern sales negotiation**. Turns out that you'd be wrong more often than not.

Please keep in mind that if you take a look at the negotiation definition, you'll see that a sales negotiation is all about power – who has it and who doesn't. One way that the other side of the table can **gain power** during your next negotiation is to make you feel physically threatened.

Now I'm not saying that they'll jump you in the parking lot before you show up to negotiate, although that might do the trick. Instead, physical intimidation can take on a lot of different, more **subtle forms** that you need to be aware of.

The first way that the other side may try to physically intimidate you is through their lead negotiator. **Is this person physically large?** How close to you are they sitting? Do they swing their hands a lot during the negotiation in a way that causes them to come close to you?

The next level of physical intimidation is associated with who is on the other side's team. How many people do they have – having an excessively large negotiating team is **a form of physical intimidation**. Are there members of their team who don't seem to play any role? Do these people spend their time just staring at you or members of your team? Remember, their role is probably to throw you off of your negotiating game and cause power to transfer to the other team.

Environmental Intimidation During A Negotiation

As though physical intimidation wasn't enough, another tactic that may be employed by the other side during a sales negotiation is **environmental intimidation**. This happens when the other side manipulates the negotiating environment in order to make it harder for you to focus on the negotiations.

One of the easiest ways to do this is to **increase the temperature in the negotiating room**. If you show up for a negation wearing a suit and discover the other side sitting there in short sleeved shirts with no jacket on, you can pretty much assume that they are planning on cranking the heat during the meeting.

Another approach is to **lock the door** in which you are conducting your negotiations. This is a meaningless gesture, but it can cause a dramatic distraction for your team during the negotiations.

Finally, sitting your team on the side of a negotiating table that faces large windows **in which the sun will either be rising or setting** can cause you discomfort and distract you from the deal that is being hammered out.

What All Of This Means For You

It's a fact of life that when the other side of the table is thinking about how they can get the best deal out of their next negotiation with you, they may decide to use either physical or environmental intimidation tactics to get their way. **No matter what is being negotiated, you need to come prepared for this**.

Physical intimidation does not require the other side to actually assault you. This type of tactic will work for the other side if you even think that you may be **at a physical risk during the negotiations**. Environmental intimidation tactics can also be subtle – you may just feel uncomfortable during the negotiations and not know why.

Whenever you find either of these tactics being used against you, **you need to take action**. The other side can't get the deal that they are looking for if you don't participate in the negotiations and so you can control the level of intimidation. Treat the negotiation as a principled negotiation and cause the other side to halt the intimidation and address the issue before you'll agree to continue negotiating. This way you'll be showing them who's really the boss.

Chapter 8

Negotiating: Men vs. Women – Who Wants To Win More?

Chapter 8: Negotiating: Men vs. Women – Who Wants To Win More?

In the world of negotiations there is a classic question that has existed since the start of time: **who wants to "win" a negotiation more, men or women?** I've heard this one debated over countless meals in countless bars over the years and yet I've never hear a good answer. We all have different negotiation styles and negotiating techniques, who does it better? Guess what: that's all changed now. The researchers have completed their study and now we know the answer.

Who Needs Ethics?

Researchers have recently published in the Journal of Experimental Social Psychology the results of their studies on the differences between men and women when something is being negotiated. **The results are not pretty.**

What the researchers found was that it appears that all too often, during the negotiation process men were willing to put their ethical standards aside during a negotiation in order to win. So much for the negotiation definition that says that we're all supposed to be conducting a principled negotiation. The reason for this behavior was that men were **more pragmatic in how they reasoned about ethics**. This mean that they could be more lenient in how they went about applying ethical standards. To use a big word, the researchers discovered that men were more prone to what the researchers called a "moral hypocrisy".

Why Each Negotiation Means So Much To A Man

As though that all wasn't enough, the researchers found something else out. They discovered that during a negotiation, men more often than not tend to **assume that their masculinity is at stake**. They will take some very specific actions because of this.

Specifically, they will view the negotiation as a threat and this will cause them to **act more aggressively**. In order to be successful during the negotiation and to protect their masculinity, men are willing to use ethics as just another negotiating tool.

What All Of This Means For You

Finally we appear to **have an answer** to the classic question of who wants to win a negotiation more: men or women. The researchers have completed their study and they say that the answer is men.

However, it turns out that the reason that the scientists were able to come to this conclusion was because their study revealed that men are more willing to **relax their ethical standards** when they are involved in a negotiation. They also assume that their masculinity is at stake during the negotiation and this can make them more aggressive.

The next time that you are involved in a negotiation, make sure that you **know which gender is sitting on the other side of the table**. Knowing this may help you to come up with a strategy that will result in a better deal for both sides.

Chapter 9

Tips For Conducting High-Stress Negotiations

Chapter 9: Tips For Conducting High-Stress Negotiations

Not all negotiations are the same. Some can make you feel **a great deal of stress**: perhaps large financial terms are being negotiated or a big business deal is being put together. When your stress level goes up, a different style of negotiating is called for.

It's All About The Big Picture

The last thing that any of us want to do is to enter into a negotiation where we have an incomplete, or even worse, an incorrect view **of what the other side of the table wants to get out of the negotiation**. In cases like this, the negotiation styles and negotiating techniques that you normally use may not work. Instead of proceeding based on our assumptions or our best guesses, we need to take the time to find out from the other side what they want to accomplish before the negotiation begins. Once you know this, you can use it to shape your objectives – and figure out if you're going to be able to achieve them.

When starting a negotiation, you are going to want to avoid going in with an assumption that you know everything that you need to know. Instead, take the time to **ask the other side questions** about how they see the situation that is being negotiated. All negotiators need to be careful to not make assumptions about the other side. If we allow ourselves to believe that we have entered into the negotiations with no biases, then we're just going to be fooling ourselves.

Finally, we always need to be careful about how we view the other side of the table. It's almost instinctive for us to assume that **they are plotting against us**. If we see them as being nefarious, then we're going to end up interacting with them that way. A better approach is to come into the negotiations with an open mind. This will always lead you to a better outcome.

Discover What's Going On And Then Collaborate

We all **react to stress differently**. More often than not, when we find ourselves in a stressful negotiation, we adopt a posture that we believe will make us look threating to the other side. By doing this we feel that we are now more in control of the proceedings. It turns out that we're not really in charge at all.

When we are feeling this way, we tend to **over react**. We take extreme negotiating positions and we start to make excessive demands of the other side from the start of the negotiations. When we do this, the other side will react. They will start to show resistance and very quickly the negotiations will dissolve into some form of a stalemate.

Instead, what we need to do is to is at the start **find out what is important to the other side** – and why. In order to prevent a stalemate from happening, what you are going to have to do is to is to make proposals to the other side and then ask the other side for their critique – what would they change in order to make it better?

What All Of This Means For You

Every principled negotiation that we engage in **is different**. The ones that cause us the most stress are the ones in which the most is riding on us being able to reach a deal with the other side of the table.

In order to be successful in these negotiating situations **we need a different set of negotiating skills**. The first thing that we need to do is to make sure that we have a good understanding of the overall picture of the situation being negotiated. Next we can take time to learn what the other side of the table's true motivations are and then propose multiple solutions to them.

As stressful as some negotiations can be, the good news is that **we can still be successful in these tasks**. Taking the time to learn the negotiating skills that we need to deal with these situations will allow us to be successful in even the most stressful negotiating situations.

Chapter 10

Extreme Negotiating: How To Do Your Best When Under Pressure

Chapter 10: Extreme Negotiating: How To Do Your Best When Under Pressure

Those of us who deal in the world of negotiations know that **not all negotiations are created equal**. One of the biggest differences is the amount of pressure that we find ourselves under during the negotiation. The bigger the stakes are, the more pressure that we feel that we are under. How we deal with all of that pressure is what separates the good negotiators from everyone else...

How To Get Real Buy-In From The Other Side

High pressure negotiations can cause us to **change how we behave** — we often start to use different negotiation styles and negotiating techniques. When the pressure goes up, it is a very natural reaction for us to start to play hardball with the other side of the table. This can even lead us to start to use coercion in order to make deals happen.

There is a downside to us behaving this way. The other side of the table **will react to our behavior in a negative way**. What will happen is that they will start to resent us and our negotiation style. This is going to lead to conflicts later on in the negotiations. If we have to negotiate with the other side of the table again in the future, then those negotiations are going to be that much more difficult.

In order to get real buy-in from the other side, take the time to **appeal to their sense of fairness**. Ask them "what should we do to resolve this situation?" Try to appeal to logic and legitimacy and keep in mind that they are going to have to be able to justify any decision that they make to their critics after the negotiations are done.

It's All About Trust

Time always seems to be in a limited supply when the stakes are high in a pressure filled negotiation. If we're not careful, we may end up taking the quick & easy path in order to make progress in the negotiation. This is almost always a bad idea.

It may seem like a good idea to **trade resources** in order to get the other side of the table to do things that we need them to do. We may be tempted to do this because we don't have a lot of time to spend on the negotiation. However, all too often what then happens is that the other side of the table starts to extort us for more resources or they now disrespect us.

Instead of trying to **buy a good relationship with the other side** using resources, instead take the time to find out why a breakdown in trust has occurred and start to look for ways to fix it. Treat concessions as valuable items. Only make them if your team didn't do something that was promised or if commitments were somehow broken. Always treat the other side of the table with respect and you'll earn their respect.

What All Of This Means For You

Pressure is a part of all of our lives. During a principled negotiation, pressure is always going to be there. However, there will be some negotiations in which pressure **plays a significant role** – we really care about how the negotiation comes out and we can feel the pressure growing.

In order keep the negotiations on track, one of the first things that you need to do is to **get genuine buy-in** from the other side of the table. This will help them to defend their decisions to their critics after the negotiations are over. Taking the time to deal with any relationship issues at the start of the negotiations will boost trust and cooperation during the negotiations.

Nobody likes to have to **operate under a lot of pressure**. However, if we realize that this is just a fact of life in some of our negotiations, then we can focus on finding ways of dealing with it. Use these suggestions and you'll be able to get more out of your next high-pressure negotiation.

Chapter 11

Testing Is What Good Negotiators Do Best

Chapter 11: Testing Is What Good Negotiators Do Best

I'm not sure how you felt about testing back when you were in school, but I can tell you that I really didn't like it. However, I've put that all behind me now that I negotiate. It turns out that **testing is something that every negotiator needs to be good at** even if that means that you've got to go back to school. Read on and I'll explain myself.

Test The Other Side's Negotiating Skills

I've got some news for you that I suspect that you already know: in a negotiation, **a skilled negotiator will always do better than an unskilled negotiator**. The reason for this should be pretty clear. A skilled negotiator is going to know more about tactics, countermeasures, and strategies that will be required to reach a favorable outcome.

What this means for you is that when a negotiation starts, you are going to have to be **constantly testing the other side of the table**. Try a tactic and see how they react. Employ a countermeasure to one of their moves and see if they implement a countermeasure to your countermeasure. If you find that they are matching your negotiation styles and negotiating techniques, then you'll know that you are up against a tough competitor. If they don't seem to understand what you are doing, then you just may have the upper hand in this negotiation.

Test The Resolve Of The Other Side

Just exactly **how firm is the other side of the table's position** on any given issue in a negotiation? Although it may appear that they are inflexible on a given negotiation point, always take the time to test their resolve.

The simple fact is that you'll never know how flexible they are willing to be **until you test them**. The truth of the matter is that the other side may also not know how much resolve they have on an issue until you start to push them on it. They may not know how many concessions that they will be willing to make until you ask for them.

What All Of This Means For You

It turns out that testing is not something that is only done in schools. Every negotiator needs to be willing to go into their next principled negotiation **ready to test the other side**.

This kind of negotiation testing **can take on many different forms**. It can be as simple as testing the skills of the other side by using a tactic and observing how they react to it. It can be a bit more complex as you test their resolve and discover how many concessions they are going to be willing to make to you.

In the end we all need to realize just exactly **what the testing that is done during a negotiation is**: it is a way of collecting more information about the negotiation. If you can lean to do this type of testing well, then you'll earn high marks during your next negotiation!

Chapter 12

Do You Have The Personality Needed For Negotiation?

Chapter 12: Do You Have The Personality Needed For Negotiation?

Quick: define what you think **the perfect negotiation** would be. What came into your mind? Did you see yourself showing up at the bargaining table, laying out your demands, getting agreement from the other side of the table, and then going home? Bad news if that is your dream because it's never going to happen that way.

What Should Your Goal For Your Next Negotiation Be?

If you were ever to show up for a negotiation, state your demands, and have the other side of the table agree with you – watch out! What this means is that you could have gotten a better deal! A good negotiation always takes time.

If you want to be successful in your next negotiation, then you need to enter the negotiations with goals. Among these goals you need to include the desire to be able to reach out to the other side and **sympathize with their situation**. They have pressures and demands are being placed on them and you need to be able to understand their situation.

Additionally, you need to be able to create a real interest in **them in reaching a deal with you**. Any negotiation where only one side is seeking to reach a deal will never be successful. Instead, what needs to happen is that both sides need to have the goal of creating a real interest in each other and allow this interest to flow back and forth during the negotiations.

What Kind Of Personality Do You Need In Order To Negotiate?

In the end, this all comes down to **the type of personality** that you are willing to bring to your next negotiation. A great deal of the personality that you'll be able to bring to the table has to do with how the other side sees you when you first show up.

What this means for you is that you are going to have to take the time to **convince them about your qualifications** to conduct this negotiation before the negotiations start. Your ultimate goal needs to be to convince the decision makers on the other side of the table that you are going to be able to do what you'll promise that you can do during the negotiations.

The personality that you'll be able to bring to the table will be greatly influenced by **how the other side views you**. If you've been able to provide them with the proof that you'll be able to carry out what you promise them that you'll do during the negotiations, then they'll accept you as a person that they can do a deal with. The ability to demonstrate to the other side that you truly mean what you tell them will allow what you say during the negotiations to be believed.

What Does All Of This Mean For You?

In order to be successful in your next principled negotiation, you are going to have to have the personality that is required to **connect with the other side of the table**. If you think that you're just going to show up and get the other side to agree to your demands, then you're in for a rude surprise!

In order to be successful in a negotiation, you need to be able to convince the other side that you both **care about them** and that you have a real interest in them being successful. In order to do this, you need to take the time to convince the other side that you have the necessary qualifications before the negotiations even start. Let them know that you can do what you promise to do during the negotiations.

Given all of the negotiation styles and negotiating techniques that get used during a typical negotiation, it can be very easy to forget the role that your personality will play in getting you the deal that you are looking for. Take the time to **connect with the other side of the table** and you'll improve your chances of reaching a deal that both sides can live with.

Hard work does not guarantee success; However, success does not happen without hard work.

- Dr. Jim Anderson

Create An Effective Negotiating Team At Your Company!

Dr. Jim Anderson is available to provide training and coaching on the topics that are the most important to people who have to negotiate: how can my team effectively prepare for and execute a successful negotiation that will get us what we both want and need?

Dr. Anderson believes that in order to both learn and remember what he says, audiences need to laugh. Each one of his speeches is full of fun and humor so that what he says "sticks" with everyone.

Dr. Anderson's Negotiating Training Includes:

1. How to plan for a negotiation: what information do you need and where can you find it?

2. What's the best way to explore how a deal can be created during a negotiation?

3. How can you bring a negotiation to a close without giving in to the other side?

Dr. Jim Anderson works with over 100 customers per year. To invite Dr. Anderson to work with you, contact him at:

Phone: 813-418-6970 or
Email: jim@BlueElephantConsulting.com

Photo Credits:

Cover - Laurenz Bobke
https://www.flickr.com/photos/travelphotos/

Chapter 1 - What What
https://www.flickr.com/photos/whatwhat/

Chapter 2 - Álvaro Tajada Portalo
https://www.flickr.com/photos/altapor/

Chapter 3 - Bill Norton
https://www.flickr.com/photos/blnk8/

Chapter 4 - nestor ferraro
https://www.flickr.com/photos/nestorferraro/

Chapter 5 - Patrick Ruddy
https://www.flickr.com/photos/11571626@N00/

Chapter 6 - Pictures of Money
https://www.flickr.com/photos/pictures-of-money/

Chapter 7 - Hans Splinter
https://www.flickr.com/photos/archeon/

Chapter 8 - Jason Pratt
https://www.flickr.com/photos/jasonpratt/

Chapter 9 - Abie Sudiono
https://www.flickr.com/photos/abiesudiono/

Chapter 10 - Kayla Sawyer
https://www.flickr.com/photos/ksawyer/

Chapter 11 – essenj
https://www.flickr.com/photos/ajaffer/

Chapter 12 – THOR
https://www.flickr.com/photos/geishaboy500/

Other Books By The Author

Product Management

- What Product Managers Need To Know About World-Class Product Development: How Product Managers Can Create Successful Products

- How Product Managers Can Learn To Understand Their Customers: Techniques For Product Managers To Better Understand What Their Customers Really Want

- Product Management Secrets: Techniques For Product Managers To Boost Product Sales And Increase Customer Satisfaction

- Product Development Lessons For Product Managers: How Product Managers Can Create Successful Products

- Customer Lessons For Product Managers: Techniques For Product Managers To Better Understand What Their Customers Really Want

- Product Failure Lessons For Product Managers: Examples Of Products That Have Failed For Product

Managers To Learn From

- Communication Skills For Product Managers: The Communication Skills That Product Managers Need To Know How To Use In Order To Have A Successful Product

- How To Have A Successful Product Manager Career: The Things That You Need To Be Doing TODAY In Order To Have A Successful Product Manager Career

- Product Manager Product Success: How to keep your product on track and make it become a success

Public Speaking

- Tools Speakers Need In Order To Give The Perfect Speech: What tools to use to create your next speech so that your message will be remembered forever!

- How To Create A Speech That Will Be Remembered

- Secrets To Organizing A Speech For Maximum Impact: How to put together a speech that will capture and hold your audience's attention

- How To Become A Better Speaker By Changing How You Speak: Change techniques that will transform a speech into a memorable event

- How To Give A Great Presentation: Presentation techniques that will transform a speech into a memorable event

- How To Rehearse In Order To Give The Perfect Speech: How to effectively rehearse your next speech to that your message be remembered forever!

- Secrets To Creating The Perfect Speech: How to create a speech that will make your message be remembered forever!

- Secrets To Organizing The Perfect Speech: How to organize the best speech of your life!

- Secrets To Planning The Perfect Speech: How to plan to give the best speech of your life

- How To Show What You Mean During A Presentation: How to use visual techniques to transform a speech into a memorable event

CIO Skills

- Becoming A Powerful And Effective Leader: Tips And Techniques That IT Managers Can Use In Order To Develop Leadership Skills

- CIO Secrets For Growing Innovation: Tips And Techniques For CIOs To Use In Order To Make Innovation Happen In Their IT Department

- Your Success As A CIO Depends On How Well You Communicate: Tips And Techniques For CIOs To Use In Order To Become Better Communicators

- What CIOs Need To Know About Working With Partners: Techniques For CIOs To Use In Order To Be Able To Successfully Work With Partners

- Critical CIO Management Skills: Decision Making Skills That Every CIO Needs To Have In Order To Be Able To Make The Right Choices

- How CIOs Can Make Innovation Happen: Tips And Techniques For CIOs To Use In Order To Make Innovation Happen In Their IT Department

- CIO Communication Skills Secrets: Tips And Techniques For CIOs To Use In Order To Become Better Communicators

- Managing Your CIO Career: Steps That CIOs Have To Take In Order To Have A Long And Successful Career

- CIO Business Skills: How CIOs can work effectively with the rest of the company!

IT Manager Skills

- Save Yourself, Save Your Job – How To Manage Your IT Career: Secrets That IT Managers Can Use In Order To Have A Successful Career

- Growing Your CIO Career: How CIOs Can Work With The Entire Company In Order To Be Successful

- How IT Managers Can Make Innovation Happen: Tips And Techniques For IT Managers To Use In Order To Make Innovation Happen In Their Teams

- Staffing Skills IT Managers Must Have: Tips And Techniques That IT Managers Can Use In Order To Correctly Staff Their Teams

- Secrets Of Effective Leadership For IT Managers: Tips And Techniques That IT Managers Can Use In Order To Develop Leadership Skills

- IT Manager Career Secrets: Tips And Techniques That IT Managers Can Use In Order To Have A Successful Career

- IT Manager Budgeting Skills: How IT Managers Can Request, Manage, Use, And Track Their Funding

- Secrets Of Managing Budgets: What IT Managers Need To Know In Order To Understand How Their Company Uses Money

Negotiating

- Learn How To Signal In Your Next Negotiation: How To Develop The Skill Of Effective Signaling In A Negotiation In Order To Get The Best Possible Outcome

- Learn The Skill Of Exploring In A Negotiation: How To Develop The Skill Of Exploring What Is Possible In A Negotiation In Order To Reach The Best Possible Deal

- Learn How To Argue In Your Next Negotiation: How To Develop The Skill Of Effective Arguing In A Negotiation In Order To Get The Best Possible Outcome|

- How To Open Your Next Negotiation: How To Start A Negotiation In Order To Get The Best Possible Outcome

- Preparing For Your Next Negotiation: What You Need To Do BEFORE A Negotiation Starts In Order To Get The Best Possible Deal

- Learn How To Package Trades In Your Next Negotiation

- All Good Things Come To An End: How To Close A Negotiation - How To Develop The Skill Of Closing In Order To Get The Best Possible Outcome From A Negotiation

Miscellaneous

- The Internet-Enabled Successful School District Superintendent: How To Use The Internet To Boost Parental Involvement In Your Schools

- Power Distribution Unit (PDU) Secrets: What Everyone Who Works In A Data Center Needs To Know!

- Making The Jump: How To Land Your Dream Job When You Get Out Of College!

- How To Use The Internet To Create Successful Students And Involved Parents

How To Start A Negotiation In Order To Get The Best Possible Outcome

> This book has been written with one goal in mind – to show you how to successfully open your next negotiation. It's not easy being a negotiator and so we're going to show you how to successfully start the negotiation in a way that will get you the deal that you want!
>
> **Let's Make Your Negotiation A Success!**

What You'll Find Inside:

- **USE THE "REVERSE-GODFATHER" APPROACH TO WIN A NEGOTIATION**

- **WHY PROVIDING A "BEST AND FINAL OFFER" IS NEVER A GOOD IDEA**

- **NEGOTIATING: MEN VS. WOMEN – WHO WANTS TO WIN MORE?**

- **DO YOU HAVE THE PERSONALITY NEEDED FOR NEGOTIATION?**

Dr. Jim Anderson brings his 25 years of real-world experience to this book. He's been a negotiator at some of the world's largest firms. He's going to show you what you need do (and not do!) in order to get the best deal out of your next negotiation!

www.ingramcontent.com/pod-product-compliance
Lightning Source LLC
Chambersburg PA
CBHW060419190526
45169CB00002B/976